Treasures (

Mythology

Tales Of Roman Gods, Heroes, And Mythological Creatures

(Learn About One Of The Most Fascinating Civilizations In The History Of The World)

Austin D. Kaplan

Bluesource And Friends

This book is brought to you by Bluesource And Friends, a happy book publishing company.

Our motto is **"Happiness Within Pages"**

We promise to deliver amazing value to readers with our books.

We also appreciate honest book reviews from our readers.

Connect with us on our Facebook page www.facebook.com/bluesourceandfriends and stay tuned to our latest book promotions and free giveaways.

Don't forget to claim your FREE books!

Brain Teasers:

https://tinyurl.com/karenbrainteasers

Harry Potter Trivia:

https://tinyurl.com/wizardworldtrivia

Sherlock Puzzle Book (Volume 2)

https://tinyurl.com/Sherlockpuzzlebook2

Also check out our other books

"67 Lateral Thinking Puzzles"

https://tinyurl.com/thinkingandriddles

"Rookstorm Online Saga"

https://tinyurl.com/rookstorm

"Korman's Prayer"

https://tinyurl.com/kormanprayer

"The Convergence"

https://tinyurl.com/bloodcavefiction

"The Hardest Sudokos In Existence (Ranked As The Hardest Sudoku Collection Available In The Western World)"

https://tinyurl.com/MasakiSudoku

DESCRIPTION 10

INTRODUCTION 14

CHAPTER 1: AN OVERVIEW OF THE ROMAN PEOPLES AND CULTURES 17

PART I: GODS AND GODDESSES 27

CHAPTER 2: SATURNALIA: CELEBRATING THE MAKING OF THE WORLD 30

CHAPTER 3: JUPITER AND JUNO: PATERNAL AND MATERNAL FORCES 37

CHAPTER 4: LOVE AND WAR/VENUS AND MARS 42

CHAPTER 5: DEITIES OF LAND AND OF SEA .49

CHAPTER 6: DEITIES OF MIND AND MATTER 56

PART II: CULTURE AND LEGENDS 63

CHAPTER 7: THE FOUNDING OF ROME: THE BOY-WOLVES ROMULUS AND REMUS 66

CHAPTER 8: EPIC TALES: THE AENEID 72

CHAPTER 9: EPIC TALES: THE METAMORPHOSES 79

CHAPTER 10: THE SENATE: ROME AS DEMOCRACY **86**

CHAPTER 11: THE EMPERORS: ROME AS EMPIRE **92**

PART III: MONSTERS AND HEROES..............**99**

CHAPTER 12: HUMAN-ANIMAL HYBRIDS: FIENDS AND FRIENDS..................................... **103**

CHAPTER 13: FEMALE FIGURES, TRAGIC TEMPTRESSES **109**

CHAPTER 14: THE TWELVE TASKS OF HERCULES **116**

CHAPTER 15: AUGUSTUS CAESAR AND THE GOLDEN AGE... **126**

CHAPTER 16: CONTEMPORARY CHARACTERS: ROMAN HEROES OF POP CULTURE............. **134**

CHAPTER 17: OTHER ENCHANTING STORIES & FIGURES.. **138**

CONCLUSION **144**

Association, and should be considered as legally binding within the United States.

The reproduction, transmission, and duplication of any of the content found herein, including any specific or extended information, will be done as an illegal act regardless of the end form the information ultimately takes. This includes copied versions of the work, both physical, digital and audio, unless express consent of the publisher is provided beforehand. Any additional rights reserved.

Furthermore, the information that can be found within the pages described forthwith shall be considered both accurate and truthful when it comes to the recounting of facts. As such, any use, correct or incorrect, of the provided information will render the publisher free of responsibility as to the actions taken outside of their direct purview. Regardless, there are zero scenarios where the original author or the publisher can be deemed liable in any fashion for any

Description

Enter a world where gods and goddesses mingle with the humans that worship them in elaborate temples, where heroes fight epic battles and monsters are thwarted, where legendary tales are told with an eye toward eternal glory—the treasure that is Roman mythology is an undeniable pleasure to read. Explore another world of ancient values, virtues, and vices, which are never to be forgotten.

The motifs of Roman mythology are similar to that of many other mythologies: Supernatural power is a handy way to explain the extraordinary; heroes are larger-than-life, with superhuman strength and wisdom to spare; gods are tricky and should be approached with caution; harrowing journeys are undertaken; battles are fought and champions are forged. The Romans developed a highly-sophisticated government and military, and successfully conquered much of the known Western world; their influence is undeniable still yet today. We can see the Roman evolution from their legendary founding, to their epic expansion, to their continued presence in our popular imagination through the thread of their treasure trove of myths and tales.

This book can take you through that journey, beginning with an overview of the Roman peoples and cultures, and into an understanding of their pantheon of gods and goddesses, their amazing tales of adventure and restless search for meaning, and a glimpse into who they actually were via the stories they held dear. Some specific elements you will encounter:

- Some of the main gods of the Greco-Roman pantheon, with all their quirks and foibles
- The Roman Council of Twelve Gods and their all-too-human role in the peoples they oversee
- The epic tales of the founding of one of the greatest empires in history

- The multiple myths of the *Metamorphoses*, from tales of transformation to love stories, both tragic and magical

- The politics and history of Rome that informed the stories the ancient Romans told about themselves and their culture

- From the Minotaur to the Medusa— fascinating human-animal hybrids

- The vision of women in Roman culture, from temptress to protector

- Stories about one of the most legendary figures in mythological history: Hercules

- The first Roman emperor and his desire to create a new story of Rome

- Contemporary visions of Roman characters and how they inform our Western institutions, our literary and artistic history, and our contemporary culture

Roman mythology is diverse and fascinating, offering us an insight into how ancient people believed and lived, into what they valued and vilified, and into how they loved and thrived. Finally, if you have enjoyed these treasured tales of Roman mythology, don't forget to explore the other fantastic realms of mythological magic in this series of books: *Treasures of Egyptian Mythology*, *Treasures of Celtic Mythology*, *Treasures of Norse Mythology*, and *Treasures of Greek Mythology*. You will find yourself in awe of the sweeping scope of history and culture represented by these mythological traditions, as well as get a better understanding of how we continually make and re-make these myths for our own times. That's the fabulous thing about myths: They never truly die.

Introduction

Undoubtedly, the Romans loom large in the popular imagination. From *Spartacus* and *Cleopatra* to Russel Crowe's *Gladiator* and HBO's *Rome*, popular culture has made entertaining use of Roman mythology. The real history and mythology, as it turns out, is even more fascinating than the film and television interpretations. It is hard to say, definitively, who the Roman people were, especially as the empire grew— many peoples of many different cultures were ultimately absorbed into this far-flung and powerful empire. Still, there were certain elements of Roman culture that remained distinctly Roman, and its legacy is undeniably yet present.

The motifs of Roman mythology, in general, are similar to that of many other mythologies: Magic is a handy way to explain the extraordinary; heroes are larger-than-life, with strength and wisdom to spare; gods are tricky and should be approached with caution; harrowing journeys are undertaken; battles are fought and warriors are forged. There is always the constant reminder of the fragility of life, in the fear over land and harvest, destiny and fate. Loyalty and bravery and sacrifice are tantamount; there is also a hefty dose of wit and wisdom, the chicanery needed to fool the gods or deceive an enemy, and the smarts to know how best to hold onto land and power. Not to mention the unquenching thirst for adventure, and the desire to achieve everlasting glory.

From the Roman pantheon of deities—largely borrowed from the Greeks—to the substantial and lasting impact of the Roman Empire, Roman mythology offers an array of exciting adventure, heroic exploits, and time-honored tales. So, embark upon these stories with the verve of SPQR, still engraved on city markers throughout Rome: The Senate and People of Rome. Gathered herein are the collective tales of the many peoples of this rich and vibrant culture.

CHAPTER 1: An Overview of the Roman Peoples and Cultures

The influence of Roman culture, its past empire, and its vast mythology reverberate throughout the Western world. While Greece was the original inspiration behind many of Rome's greatest myths, and certainly behind its pantheon of gods, Rome was, itself, a unique culture that fostered one of the longest-lasting and most influential empires in history. One of the reasons for the unparalleled success of the Roman Empire was that there was an underlying policy of inclusion—to a degree—within Roman culture. That is, if you were conquered by Rome, you simply had to follow a basic set of Roman cultural mores in order to become a citizen: So, when we, today, speak of the "Roman peoples," we are not simply speaking of the ancestors of modern-day Italians, but also of French, Spanish, Greek, African, and other peoples who became a part of the greater empire. As well, because Rome's dominance over the Western world endured for many centuries, the character of Roman culture changes over time.

The center of Roman culture was always firmly rooted in the city of Rome itself—the largest city of the ancient world for many decades with million people or more residing in the city itself. It was arranged around the seven hills—from the wealthy Palatine Hill to the gritty Aventine Hill—and became organized as a central city a few hundred years before the birth of Christ. The founding of Rome has created an enduring myth of the boys, Romulus and Remus, who were allegedly raised by wolves. You can discover more information on that tale in Chapter 7.

The achievements of ancient Roman civilization are truly remarkable. They completed feats of engineering hitherto unknown in the Western world—in particular, the construction of the aqueducts which allowed fresh running water into homes and public baths, as well as enabled a sewer system to rival many modern set-ups. In addition, paved roads were a trait of the Roman Empire, and made travel between provinces easy—thus bestowing a great advantage on an empire that was still growing. There was also the cultivating of the Roman alphabet—the very alphabet that right now enables you to read this text—and the creation of the Roman calendar, again still in use in much of the Western world. The Roman Senate was, while it lasted, the most refined political institution of its day, and would inspire republics throughout history—ours included.

Lest we not forget the architectural accomplishments, it would be impossible to imagine Rome without the magisterial image of the Coliseum. Construction began under Emperor Vespasian in 72 CE, and was completed eight years later. Holding between 50,000 and 80,000 people, there was no other stadium to equal it for hundreds of years. But the Coliseum is only one of the many monuments that dot the Roman landscape, such as the Trajan's Column, detailing the many victories of Rome during the Dacian wars, and the Pantheon, which was once a temple to the ancient gods, and now stands as a Christian church. You can also find the faint remains of the Circus Maximus, on which chariot races and other sporting entertainments were held. There are also remains of the ancient aqueducts, and other palaces sprinkled throughout the territory of the former Roman Empire.

Roman visual art was defined by its Greek roots, for the most part: Marble carvings and statues, the use of colored tiles in mosaic floors, ceilings, and walls, and the widespread production of pottery. The same could also be said of Rome's great literature: *The Aeneid*, the epic poem that depicts the founding of the Roman Empire after the fall of Troy, essentially picks up where *The Iliad* and *The Odyssey*—the foundational texts of Greek civilization—leave off. This is not to say that Roman art was derivative; it was merely very closely affiliated with the other great pillar of Western civilization, Greece, in its politics and religion as well as its art.

Last, but certainly not least, Roman culture was one of wine and food. In fact, much of the impetus for the continuing expansion of the empire was, indeed, about procuring enough victuals for its growing population. Egypt was called the "bread basket" of the Roman Empire, and without its grain, the city could not have thrived. While the popular, and usually unflattering, image of the Roman feast is surely exaggerated, it was certainly a staple at festival times and religious holidays. The wine was always watered down to temper both its potency and its (sometimes harsh) taste. Those who drank their wine without water were suspected of being intemperate—a charge that carried more weight later in imperial times, with the onset of the Augustan-era morals.

In the early days of Rome, the culture was very much Hellenistic in the structure—that is, it followed the same kind of rules and organization that the Greeks had followed, just as it followed Greece in art, architecture, and religion. One truly Roman trait—though of course this was also practiced by the Greeks—was the central importance of the family, and a very patriarchal-structured one at that. All societies recognize the importance of family to varying degrees, but for the ancient Romans, it became almost a cult of devotion. Under the first true Roman emperor, Augustus, laws regarding how families interacted and were recognized became strictly regulated. The debauchery that we often associate with ancient Rome is almost certainly the product of Hollywood, and while it is certainly the case that some emperors were ethically corrupt and morally bankrupt, it is even more true that many emperors felt that they upheld the highest of Roman values: They were like a father figure for all of society, guiding them to greatness and, as in the regular family, the absolute ruler over all his children. This was excellent for central organization and clarity, but not always so wonderful for certain segments of society.

Women were not granted the same status as men, and foreigners, while welcomed to a degree, were often barred from many professions. Of course, we must also mention that Rome harbored and sanctioned an enormous population of slaves—this is one of the reasons that such great monuments were completed at the time, as well as why Rome needed to secure other territories to feed its peoples. Some estimates suggest that the enslaved population of Rome reached more than 25 percent at times.

While there was a shift in the general culture of Rome, this came with a shift in the political structure of Rome. When we remember Rome, we often talk primarily about the "fall of the Roman Empire," but for much of its history, Rome was, in fact, a republic. It wasn't quite the democracy that we practice today, but it was certainly almost unique in history (the Greeks tried it first, as with many things). Rome was ruled by a senate of wealthy Roman men for centuries until corruption and war and various other factors weakened its rule. Julius Caesar was the first to try a whole-scale grab at sole power, but he was limited in his success. It would be his nephew, Augustus Caesar, who would consolidate power, become the first Roman emperor, and eventually declare himself a deity. The Senate remained, but it became merely a symbol of a bygone era, and not a functioning political party. You can read more about this evolution of ancient Rome in Part II.

The height of the Roman Empire would mean that Latin would become the lingua franca of the Western world for centuries—really, it wasn't until the 18th century that Latin was replaced by English as the language spoken around the world. Scholars who wanted to be taken seriously published in Latin many centuries after the fall of the empire, and this so-called "dead" language is still taught in grammar schools, religious institutions, and centers of learning the world over.

The fall of Rome in around the 5th century CE precipitated a catastrophic decline in literacy rates and artistic, archeological, and mathematical achievements. The centralized system that was the Roman Empire gave way to small fiefdoms with various warring civilizations vying for power—what some historians call the "Dark Ages," though others find the phrase misleading and pejorative. It wasn't until the Renaissance of the 14th and 15th centuries CE that many of the innovations that had been discovered and utilized during Roman times were reclaimed, such as the aqueduct, adequate roads, and even the ability to build domes that began again to cap the most famous structures in the world, such as St. Peter's Basilica and the Duomo in Florence. While Rome certainly had its shortcomings and imperfections, it was a beacon of light in the ancient world, where peoples from all over could look for learning, for art, and for political and military inspiration.

PART I: Gods and Goddesses

The pantheon of Roman gods and goddesses is derived, in a large part, from the Greek canon. However, the Roman myths put a slightly different spin on certain characters, reflecting a different cultural outlook. In addition, the lasting popularity of these myths and figures is undeniable, given the ubiquitous presence of Roman themes and figures in many modern-day incarnations.

The gods who appear with frequency happen to be many-skilled and brave warriors, like Jupiter and Mars, who you will read about below. Roman mythology tends to favor the powerful, especially in the time of the empire, and the expansion of Roman power throughout Europe. One of the hallmarks about gods and goddesses throughout Greco-Roman mythology is that they are representations of particular ideas that their respective societies held at the time—and, as such, are very human in nature. In fact, this canon of mythology is perhaps the most anthropomorphized of the popular mythological traditions. Gods and goddesses don't simply witness events from above or beyond; they are active participants in the said events and work to manipulate the interactions of humans and the events of human history. Also, many of the tales that introduce us to the gods and goddesses change over time in order to meet society's different needs at different moments—this is true for virtually all mythological traditions.

The tales surrounding the gods and goddesses of Roman mythology—as is also common with all mythologies—are usually stories that either seek to confirm a common cultural ideal, or work to provide a cautionary function—that is, myths are told to remind us of who we are, where we come from, and attempt to preserve the goodness of a particular way of life. On the other hand, myths can be told like parables, warning us against the dangers of going against a particular value or cultural norm. When we read these tales in contemporary times, we may not always agree on the "goodness" of that way of life, because our value systems are probably different. But they still give us an insight into what heroism and triumph or villainy and trial meant to a certain people at a certain time. As such, they are fascinating to read—and to learn from—giving us a window into an ancient culture that is so very different from our own.

The gods and goddesses of these myths are likewise designed either to represent an ideal to which humans should aspire—a role model of sorts—or to discourage certain types of behavior. Still, being gods and goddesses, they can be fickle and changeable, not always to be trusted or not always to be feared. They remain figures of awe and reverence because of their supernatural gifts and abilities, regardless of their actions, and the power that they seemingly have over humans inspires us to return again and again to their marvelous stories.

CHAPTER 2: Saturnalia: Celebrating the Making of the World

Saturn was considered the father of the gods, the bringer of life and the god of harvest and abundance. It was said that Saturn ruled over the land of Rome before the city itself was founded, so he became associated with one of the most important festivals on the Roman calendar—Saturnalia. He is, in fact—like most of the Roman gods and goddesses—a renaming and slight remaking of the Greek god, Chronos, who is considered the father of Time. We owe the name of our favorite weekend day, Saturday, to none other than Saturn himself (and, of course, we also got a planet out of the deal).

To understand the intricate intertwining of Greek and Roman religions is key to understanding the pantheon of Roman gods and goddesses and, in particular,

Saturn. The Romans were, at one time, a loose configuration of tribal groups, as was the case across Europe and the Mediterranean, including the Latins, Sabines, and Umbrians. There were also two distinct ethnic groups: The Etruscans to the north and the Greeks to the south. While the Etruscans left many monuments behind, they have largely been lost to history because no specific writings have ever been found; however, it is clear that they influenced early Roman culture because of the various tombs and other monuments that were left behind. In addition, they left behind the name of the famous Italian province of Tuscany. The Greeks, on the other hand, would be very influential in the creating of the Roman Republic and the pantheon of gods the people worshipped. This was, in large part, due to the conquest and occupation of parts of Greece by the Romans; this led to a syncretism between the two religious and mythological cultures that renders them nearly inseparable.

So, it is most likely true that Saturn was an older, more established god for the peoples in the area around Rome, but by the 2nd century BCE, Rome had become Hellenized (which is what the influence of Greek culture is known as). Thus, many of the traits and traditions surrounding the Greek pantheon were passed down to the Romans. To this day, we refer to most of this mythology by its compound name, Greco-Roman, because the distinguishing factors are few and far between.

Saturn, himself, belongs to a kind of pre-origin myth that runs through many mythological traditions. He was the ruler of a fabled "Golden Age," where there were peace and harmony, stability and prosperity. He did, however, have an interesting reputation of repeatedly eating his own children: This was interpreted to symbolize the cycle of time, of life and death, of rebirth and regeneration. Marcus Tullius Cicero, the renowned Roman politician, and orator put it thusly:

"By Saturn, they seek to represent that power which maintains the cyclic course of times and seasons. This is the sense that the Greek name of that god bears, for he is called <u>Kronos</u>, which is the same as <u>Chronos</u> or <u>Time</u>. Saturn, for his part, got his name because he was "sated" with years; the story that he regularly devoured his own children is explained by the fact that time devours the courses of the seasons, and gorges itself "insatiable" on the years that are past. Saturn was enchained by <u>Jupiter</u> to ensure that his circuits did not get out of control, and to constrain him with the bonds of the stars."

Saturn was, to the later Romans, the god of agriculture and the harvest. The importance of this cannot be overstated, especially to a region that would eventually hold the largest population in the Western world at one time. Without a good season and an abundant harvest, there could be widespread suffering, of course. It appears that Saturn was worshipped throughout Rome and throughout its history, with remains of temples dotting the landscape of the area.

His association with agriculture and the harvest puts him at the center of one of the largest festivals of ancient Rome—the Saturnalia. This coincided with the end of the harvest year, in December, and featured a relaxing of the social order of typical Roman life. For example, masters would serve slaves, and enormous parties would feature the mingling of people of all social classes. Feasting and revelry during this time were unparalleled: One thinks of Christmastime on the Christian calendar today. Saturn was normally portrayed throughout the year with his feet bound—perhaps referring to the strictness of his established order, or to his bound duty to keep that order—but during Saturnalia, his feet were unbound, and thus, strictures of everyday society were relaxed as well.

He is clearly associated with the order, in that he gathered together all the varying creatures—satyrs and fauns, for example—as well as the conflicting tribes, all under one civilized structure. This is a common factor in almost all mythologies: An original father figure of sorts who brings order to the chaos that is an unsettled universe. It sounds familiar to people with varying beliefs across the entire world.

One of the potentially significant differences between Saturn and the rest of the Roman pantheon is that he was worshipped, essentially, as a ceremonial god. That is, he is recognized as a figure before the time of Rome, before the establishment of the city and the kingdom, the Republic, and later the empire. The other gods and goddesses were quite real to the Roman people, in that they still existed on some other plane and were likely to interact with actual people living within Rome. Saturn was behind all of that, somehow, but he was a figurehead and remote father figure, unlike his celebrated children. For some knowledge of those, read on.

CHAPTER 3: Jupiter and Juno: Paternal and Maternal Forces

As is common in most mythologies, there is a governing couple, as it were, who look after the people that celebrate them: For Roman mythology, this is Jupiter, the king of the gods, and Juno, his wife (corresponding in Greek mythology to Zeus and Hera, respectively). Jupiter is—like Zeus before him and Thor after him—a god of thunder and the sky, and he is often depicted with a lightning bolt in his hand. He eventually came to be recognized as "Jupiter Optimus Maximus"—the best and greatest god. His wife, Juno, was the mother to the other most prominent gods and goddesses, such as Mars and Vulcan, and was recognized as "Regina Juno", or "Queen of the gods".

The origin myth of Jupiter is well known in mythological studies: It was prophesied that Saturn would devour all of his children, which, indeed, he mostly succeeded in doing. But when his wife, Ops, realized that all of her children would certainly perish in the maw of Saturn, she quickly hid Jupiter, and, instead, gave Saturn a large stone wrapped in swaddling to eat. Thus fooled, Saturn was not able, ultimately, to prevent the prophecy from coming true, and Jupiter was saved.

Later, as legend has it, Jupiter grew up to be so powerful that he made Saturn vomit up the rest of the children he had eaten, thereby single-handedly creating the Roman pantheon of gods that were worshipped during all of the ancient Roman times. His brothers and sisters then joined him in the battle—along with the Cyclopses and Giants—to overthrow Saturn and the other titans. If this story sounds familiar, it most certainly is: It is derived from the Greek mythology, and there have been a couple of iterations of *Clash of the Titans* to hit movie theaters in modern times.

Because Jupiter gets rid of the titans and his father, he is considered the greatest and best of gods. The titans were seen as monstrous and chaotic, while the next generation of gods and goddesses brought a more ordered sense to civilization. The great Temple of Jupiter in the Capitoline area of Rome was erected in the 5th century BCE, and generals and armies marched passed it in celebration of any significant victory in battle. Thus, Jupiter is associated with war, as his son Mars would also be.

Jupiter is also quite famously celebrated—or castigated—as a lusty lover who tends to embark on romantic pursuits that frequently infuriated his wife. For one famous example, Jupiter had fallen for the beautiful priestess, Io, and he decided he wanted to spend his time getting closer to her. So, he changed himself into a dark cloud—this also was to serve as a cover for the jealous Juno. Fortunately, she was not easily fooled, and upon her angry arrival to Earth, Jupiter changed Io into a white cow to protect her from Juno's ire. Eventually, he had Mercury set her free from the watchful eyes of Argus, but Juno, again, discovered his deception, and created a magical fly to sting Io for the rest of her existence. Only when Jupiter had promised not to chase Io ever again, was she set free.

Juno, for her part, was considered a mother goddess, of course, and was associated with marriage and childbirth. She was also seen as a protector of the state—perhaps this is due to her origins in older mythology than the Greek. Certainly, she is the equivalent of Hera in the Greek stories; however, there is evidence to suggest that she is much older than the time of Hellenization. Thus, she creates not only an extension of Greek mythology, but also a counter to it. Sometimes, she is depicted holding a spear and shield—quite different from the matronly depictions of Hera.

In addition, while Hera's jealousy was legendary in its ferocity and breadth, the stories regarding Juno softened within the Roman canon of myths. The overall Roman emphasis on the institution of marriage—it became absolutely sacred, with many strict laws and harsh punishments surrounding the violation of it—ultimately led to the creation of a goddess whose primary concern was the preservation and protection of women—most particularly married women. In this way, as in most mythologies, the stories that are told and the traits that are emphasized shift with the changing cultural landscape. Part of the growing Roman concern with marriage was producing citizens—real *Roman* citizens—which makes perfect sense when you consider that, as Rome expands its empire, more and more foreigners come within its purview. Thus, Juno had a significant role to fulfill in the continuation of the legacy of Roman civilization.

CHAPTER 4: Love and War/Venus and Mars

In comparison to Jupiter and Juno, who were effectively handed down from the Greek stories almost intact, Venus, and especially Mars, became more complex and manifold during their time in the Roman pantheon. Of course, Venus was the goddess of love—and also, perhaps of prostitution—and bore many children who became significant to our understanding of Roman mythology. Her brother, Mars, was the god of war, but unlike his Greek equivalent, Ares, Mars was not only the personification of a fierce warrior, but also of a judicious commander. This is in keeping with the centrality of the military to the Roman Empire—its importance cannot be overstated at the height of ancient Rome. Without Mars and the military regimens and discipline he inspired, there would have been no Roman Empire.

Venus was the goddess of love and fertility, and of desire and beauty. She has always provided great inspiration for poets and painters throughout history (think of Botticelli's world-renowned painting, *The Birth of Venus*). Venus's parentage is unknown or vague, and, like the painting, she is often depicted as emerging, fully formed, from the sea. Her Greek predecessor, Aphrodite, bears similar attributes, but the Roman presentation of Venus has surpassed the Greek goddess in reputation through the years. Venus is the embodiment of the female essence, and as such, she counterbalances the essential male traits as depicted by Mars, for example. Venus is married to Vulcan, the god of fire, and this is also key in tempering the destructive powers of the Earth (such as volcanoes). She also bore, as children, the Cupids that we still yet associate with love and Valentine's Day.

Venus, however, also bore a different role for the Romans than did Aphrodite for the Greeks. As

Roman civilization developed and expanded, Venus was essentially designated the mother of the nation: In Virgil's epic poem, *The Aeneid*, about the founding of Rome, Venus is the mother of the hero Aeneas, who survives the fall of Troy in order to reach and found Rome. This was not a mere story for the ancient Romans; this was considered historical lineage. Even Julius Caesar claimed that she was his ancestor. Thus, Venus is both a goddess of love, with temples dotting the hillsides of Rome, and worshipped throughout the empire, and a flesh-and-blood ancestor of the nation itself and its leaders.

While Venus was married to Vulcan, most of the stories regarding her love and sexual life revolve around her relationship to Mars, who was, in some accounts, actually her brother. By the time the Roman Council of 12 was established—the twelve pairings of the gods—Venus and Mars were paired just as Juno and Jupiter were. This was undoubted because Venus had the power to calm Mars's stormy temper; it was said that only Venus had the ability to soothe Mars into tranquility. Indeed, the story of Venus and Mars was enshrined in much art and literature regarding the Roman pantheon of gods, likely because their coupling provided the opportunity for neat allegories regarding the essence of male and female, of war and love. They had many offspring, including Concordia, who became the goddess of harmony in marriage and society. Most Romans turned a blind eye to the adulterous—if not incestuous—nature of their relationship.

Mars, for his part, was perhaps even more significant than Jupiter. While Jupiter was considered the father of the Olympian gods, and held some martial significance, the cult of Mars became central to the expansion of the empire, and the development of the unparalleled Roman army. While Ares, his Greek counterpart, was considered destructive and chaotic, Mars came to be seen as disciplined, and represented the value of war in preserving peace. This is clearly the result of the creation of one of the greatest armies in history: The Roman army was renowned for its discipline and the rigors of its training and fighting. In the time of imperial expansion (and, indeed, the protection of provinces and borders), the military became one of the single most important forces in Rome. Indeed, the power of Julius Caesar was derived almost exclusively from his exploits on the battlefield. Later emperors were also renowned for their expertise in the military, and it was fully acknowledged that the greatness of Rome depended more on the military than on the government. Without the military, there would be no stable empire. Without Mars, there could be, ironically, no peace.

Mars was always depicted wearing a great helmet with a spear and a shield. Thus, he symbolizes strength and warrior-like status, but also represents the dual nature of his sacred duties: The spear to fight; the shield to protect.

Mars, like Venus, also came to be wrapped up in the telling of the foundation myth of Rome. While Venus was the mother of the great hero, Aeneas, who has the honor in Virgil's epic tale, Mars was the father of the twins Romulus and Remus, who were the fabled founders of Rome in another story (see Chapters 7 and 8 for more on those foundational myths). So, Mars was venerated as a protector of Rome, as well as was the father of its peoples. Some historians argue that Mars was, in fact, the most singularly Roman of all the gods, with the rest being largely derived from Greek sources.

Temples to the God of War are built, but so are altars of peace dedicated to Mars: This complex commingling of the idea of martial might in securing domestic peace was unique to Rome in the ancient world, at least in its complexity. One can clearly hear echoes of that in our own Constitution, ensuring "domestic tranquility", while providing for "the common defense." It is no secret that the inheritance of the Greco-Roman culture has strongly reverberated throughout the Western world. The complex values that are enshrined in the figure of Mars might not be quite so foreign to us, even today.

CHAPTER 5: Deities of Land and of Sea

The rest of the gods in the Roman Council of 12 can be classified as gods of the land and sea (detailed here), or gods of the mind and otherworldly substances (as detailed in Chapter 6). The goddess Ceres is most closely associated with the land, while Diana, the huntress goddess, is also key to the Roman understanding of nature. Vulcan is the god of fire, living underground, but the myths suggest a connection to the sea as well. Of course, Neptune is the ultimate god associated with the sea and its many creatures.

Ceres is the goddess of agriculture and fertility, with Demeter as her Greek counterpart. Daughter of Saturn and sister to Jupiter, she was considered one of the most benevolent gods. Again, the importance of agriculture to pre-industrial societies was paramount:

Without the kind ministrations of Ceres, the fields would be fallow, and the people would starve. She is most often paired with her daughter, Proserpine, in the famous myth derived from Greek culture. Beautiful Proserpine is kidnapped by the god of the underworld, Pluto, separated from her mother and the other gods. Even the intervention of Jupiter would not persuade Pluto to set her entirely free. However, he allows Proserpine to visit Ceres for a certain time each year—from spring until fall. This is, of course, the time during which the crops are blooming and the fields are full, so Proserpine is associated with the arrival of spring and the regeneration of the land. The festival of Cerealia— yes, that is where the word "cereal" comes from— was held each year in the spring to honor this goddess of fruitfulness and agricultural prosperity.

Diana the Huntress is the goddess of nature, of animals, and of the moon. As such, she is a complex character, much like her Greek equivalent, Artemis.

Hunting was a central part of Roman culture, of course, and Diana is almost always pictured with her bow and arrow (think of Katniss Everdeen in *The Hunger Games*). She was a virgin goddess and thus had to be swift and strong to avoid the constant lustiness of the other gods. Ironically, she is considered also to be the goddess of childbirth and of the household, even though she herself is constantly on the move and childless. Her association with the moon is also complex: Its ever-changing phases and evocation with wildness are at odds with the depictions of her in the serene woods. Diana's manifold nature is probably the result of centuries of syncretism, wherein she blends older archetypes and various goddesses from other cultures. Thus, Diana reflects the conflicting visions of nature shared by many ancient peoples: Nature can be both benevolent (as in Ceres' nature above) or beneficial (as in the bounty of hunting), and wildly dangerous.

Vulcan, the god of fire, is associated with (of course) volcanoes, but also with forges and metal-making. He is often depicted underground, with a fiery furnace and his tools. His residence was said to be under Mount Aetna in Sicily. Portrayed as a talented blacksmith, most of the traits and stories surrounding Vulcan are indeed derived from his Greek counterpart, Hephaestus.

He is the son of Juno and Jupiter, but when he was born, he was very small and ugly—some depictions show him to be deformed—so Jupiter tossed him off the top of Mount Olympus, where he landed far down below into the sea. Belying his small size, he survived the tumble (he is a god, after all) to be raised by the sea-nymph Thetis. His childhood seems idyllic, playing with the dolphins and other sea creatures. When he finally goes ashore, he finds a lump of burning wood left behind by the fishermen, becoming immediately fascinated with it. So, he took it to a cave and learned to nurture the fire with bellows and other instruments. The extreme heat that he created could melt metal, which he could then work into weapons and jewelry. Once Juno discovered his talents, she demanded that he return to Olympus, but Vulcan refused: His home was now under the mountains and volcanoes of Earth. She was furious, so he sent her a beautiful throne upon which to sit; however, when she sat, the chair turned into a mechanical trap. She could neither move nor eat nor sleep, and was imprisoned for several days until Jupiter promised Vulcan a wife—and not just any wife, but Venus, the goddess of love and beauty. Thus, the ugliest god of them all won the most beautiful goddess via his cleverness and talent.

Lastly, Neptune, brother of Jupiter, is the powerful god of the sea. He is frequently portrayed as ill-tempered and potentially violent—much like the sea itself. After the fall of Saturn, the universe is divided among the three brothers, Jupiter, Neptune, and Pluto. Jupiter gets the sky and earth, Pluto gets the underworld, while Neptune gets the sea. In addition to his temper, he is often portrayed as a very lascivious and promiscuous god, conquering numerous nymphs of the sea, mortals of the land, and even other goddesses (including his own sister, Ceres).

Numerous myths swirl around Neptune (and his Greek counterpart, Poseidon), and he is perhaps one of the most interesting, if not always likable, god in the Greco-Roman pantheon. He is associated with dolphins in particular; the myth of how he managed to get a wife is the result of no small help from the dolphin king. He wasn't a particularly faithful husband, but the dolphin king persuaded Salacia to marry him, thinking it might tame his violent temper. Neptune is also said to be responsible for the creation of Medusa: She was once a beautiful young mortal known for her long and luscious blonde hair. Neptune caught her worshipping at the temple of Minerva, and overcome with lust, he rapes her.

Minerva decides to punish Medusa—perhaps unfairly, one might think—for desecrating her temple, thus turning her into the hideous gorgon with snakes for hair that we come to know from the myth of Perseus, in particular.

Again, as with many gods and goddesses, tales and events, Roman mythology is sometimes so closely aligned to Greek mythology that the stories and characters are virtually inseparable. This is, perhaps, the lasting strength of these stories: They transcended time and culture to secure a lasting place in our imagination to this day.

CHAPTER 6: Deities of Mind and Matter

The rest of the gods and goddesses who make up the Roman Council of 12 are: Minerva, Apollo, Mercury, and Bacchus. As with the other Roman deities, all of these have Greek counterparts, with Apollo being directly lifted from the Greeks with virtually no change at all. Minerva and Apollo are associated with skills of the intellect and the arts, while Mercury is the god of commerce and communication, and Bacchus the patron god of wine and celebration. They are loosely grouped here, as they are the deities that oversee the most daily activities of humans themselves. Rather than ruling the skies or the seas or the tumultuous fields of love and battle, these gods and goddesses help out with the skills and pleasures of everyday life.

Minerva oversees a rather long list of attributes, from wisdom and poetry, to medicine and arts. She has been often called the "goddess of a thousand works," due to her many duties. Her origin story—like her Greek counterpart, Athena—makes her well-suited to be the goddess of wisdom: Jupiter, spooked by the prophecy of his own father's demise, swallowed Minerva's mother (as Saturn had swallowed all of his other children but Jupiter, who ultimately defeated him). Undeterred, Minerva was born out of her own father's head. While this story, along with some characteristics, was passed along from the Greeks, it is generally thought that Minerva, herself, was an older god indigenous to the Etruscan culture. She was later merged, in part, with Athena in the act of syncretism, so common to the Roman canon.

Perhaps the most famous story regarding Minerva is the infamous tale of the weaving contest with the mortal girl Arachne, who declared herself better even than the goddess. Minerva's tapestry, perhaps predictably, showed scenes in which humans had dared challenge the gods and, alas, come to a sticky ending. While Arachne's tapestry was stunningly beautiful, it impiously depicted scenes of mortals who had fallen victim to the gods who had seduced them. Minerva declares herself the winner—who would have guessed otherwise?—and to punish Arachne for her boast, she turns the mortal into a spider. This is a tidy story that both explains the spider (arachnid) and its weaving abilities, as well as provide a moral about the dangers of hubris.

The god Apollo was a youthful deity—no beard and an impressive physique—and was regarded as the god of light and music, prophecy and poetry. His impressive range of oversight is just as long and varied as Minerva's. Apollo is the one significant god who came directly from the Greek pantheon without even a change of name. However, because his attributes range from the truly divine to the relatively mundane—he is both gods of light and god of archery—most scholars believe that he is the result of a merging of many different traditions to end up as one specific god to the Greco-Roman cultures. He is also sometimes depicted as a vengeful god, bringing plagues and other retributions to those who cross him, which further complicates our image of this typically beautiful god.

Mercury was the divine messenger of the gods, fostering communication between the mortals and the gods. He was the one who delivered the message to Aeneas, the epic founder of Rome, that he should leave his lover, Dido, and travel to Europe. Mercury is also depicted as changeable and mischievous—this is where we get the term "mercurial" from (a mercurial person is one who changes their mind or positions frequently, and without warning). He especially liked to trick the god Apollo, who was often so serious and solid. Mercury is also the patron god of commerce and merchants—as well as thieves: Anything to make some gold, it would seem, falls under his purview. Most of the more well-known stories about Mercury actually come originally from his Greek equivalent, Hermes. He plays an important role in the story of Jupiter's seduction of Io, warning him that his wife, Juno, would be coming to stop his affair. He was also the one who escorts Ceres's daughter, Proserpine, to the underworld. Essentially, Mercury is the impish and changeable sidekick to the more powerful gods, but his significance is always consequential. Without Mercury, the narratives of many Roman myths would not move along as smoothly.

Like Apollo, Bacchus was a god lifted almost wholly from the Greeks (even though his name was changed, unlike Apollo). His Greek counterpart, Dionysus, was the god of wine and winemaking—revelry in general. Bacchus was depicted as both the god of mysterious rituals that emphasized religious ecstasy, and outright madness. Some of the cults of Bacchus practiced very scandalous rituals, involving excessive drunkenness, violent acts, and atypically promiscuous behavior. As such, Bacchus was not always a respectable god, and his reputation greatly diminished in the years of the early empire, where a return to old-fashioned Roman values was seen as tantamount to securing its ambitions and power throughout the world stage. The festivals, routinely called "Bacchanalia", were slightly less frenzied celebrations of this type; the word itself has come to be used colloquially as a description of an excellent, if perhaps over-the-top, party.

All of the gods and goddesses in the Roman pantheon owe a debt to their Greek counterparts, and one cannot clearly or cleanly separate the two mythologies. Yet, the Romans did emphasize particular traits in the reflection of the values of the culture at a given time within their civilization. There are many more fascinating stories to be told about these gods and goddesses, the heroes they inspire (or confound), as well as about the history and culture they reflect.

PART II: Culture and Legends

Roman culture and mythology weave a tight web of mores, passing down information about how people act, how they should act, and why the world works the way it does. This is what legends, myths, and morality tales are for: To indicate to the listener (or, these days, reader) how good people behave, how bad people are punished, and thus, what values we should uphold. They are our links to the glorious and ancient past, telling us *who they were* and *what they believed*. They are also explanatory, describing how the weather works, for example, in a time before meteorology; it is no coincidence that, in all mythological traditions, there is the inevitable god of thunder (Jupiter, Lugh, Thor) and many gods of the harvest and of fertility (Ceres and Venus). These stories speculate about why certain things happen, by assigning powers to gods and other supernatural beings—this was a way of making sense of a chaotic world and understanding our place in it.

It was also a method of protection: If you pray to a certain god or goddess, or if you practice a certain ritual, or observe appropriate customs, then you will avoid suffering and will enjoy prosperity. This also serves as a way to assign responsibility elsewhere for events that happen outside of your control ("It was too wet this year for a good harvest; our offerings to Ceres weren't enough"). Concomitantly, it was a cause for celebration and feasting when events are auspicious.

Roman culture and its attendant legendary stories share many similarities with other mythological canons: Magic is all around, utilized to explain the inexplicable; heroes boast superhuman strength, sometimes with divine origins, and make good use of hard-won wisdom; gods can be trickster figures or helpers, depending on the context; adventures abound; romance is complicated and sometimes tragic; battles are forever being waged and warriors are forever being supplanted. There is always the constant reminder of the fragility of life, in the fear over land and harvest, cattle and children. Loyalty and bravery and sacrifice are tantamount; virtues that emphasize working together for the greater good are omnipresent in legendary texts. After all, without each other, we couldn't get along at all.

CHAPTER 7: The Founding of Rome: The Boy-Wolves Romulus and Remus

The legends regarding Romulus and Remus are well known and highly wrought in Roman history. The tale describes a foundational story that is both fantastically dramatic and terribly tragic. In it, Rome is founded by the most unlikely and, some might say, unlucky sons of divine parentage that you could imagine. The mythical founding of Rome in 753 BCE is one of the great stories of ancient Roman legends.

The twins Romulus and Remus were born to the daughter of a usurped king descended from the first hero of Rome, Aeneas. This daughter, Rhea Silvia, had been forced to become a Vestal Virgin—loyal to Vesta, the goddess of the hearth—after the deposing of her father, in order to avoid potential struggles for power. Vestal Virgins were not allowed to have sexual relations, and the story suggests that Rhea Silvia was either divinely visited by Mars, or taken by the demi-god, Hercules. Either way, this would mean that whatever child was born of this union could pose a threat to the kingdom, as a direct descendant of Aeneas. As well, the punishment for a Vestal Virgin who breaks her vow was death, usually by being buried alive. But the king feared that, if the child born of Rhea Silvia was in fact fathered by a god, Mars would reign down his wrath upon the kingdom. So, instead, he decreed that the mother be imprisoned, and, as it turns out, her twins, be left to die of exposure. He reasoned that the gods would show mercy on his kingdom if he spared the family a violent death. The servant who was chosen to leave the children by the Tiber River—probably to a quick and certain death, considering the elements and the animals—takes mercy on them, and puts them in a basket to float down the river.

The river god took pity on the innocent children as well, and calmed the river so that they could float gently to some sort of safety. They were first found on the riverbank by a kindly she-wolf, who suckled them when they were starving—this image, of the twin boys being suckled by a she-wolf, is ubiquitous in Rome to this day. Eventually, a shepherd and his wife took them in to raise as their own. As often happens in mythology, by random happenstance, Romulus and Remus were confronted by a group of shepherds who worked for the king that sentenced them to death. Remus was captured and taken before the king, who did not recognize the young man, while Romulus incited a group of independent shepherds to help him rescue his brother. He was able to do this, and in the ensuing scuffle, the king was killed.

The people offered Romulus and Remus the kingdom, having seen their bravery and heard of their parentage, but the twins refused it, wishing to strike out on their own. Unfortunately, the two brothers argued about the location, with Romulus preferring the Palatine Hill, and Remus choosing the Aventine Hill. They consulted an augury to see who had chosen correctly, but then argued about the results. Romulus decided to start building the walls of his city anyway, and the Palatine Hill was begun.

Remus responded by making merciless fun of what he considered to be Romulus's foolish actions. Finally, he decided to breach his brother's wall—basically, he wanted him to look weak and foolish—which angered Romulus so much that he killed his brother. Other versions, wanting to venerate both brothers, paint the murder in a different light: In one, it suggests that Remus died while breaching the wall, which simply showed that the augury favored Romulus. In another, it is suggested that Remus is killed not by his brother, but by one of his brother's supporters. In any case, as the legend stands today, Romulus is the victor, though both brothers are considered the founders, and both the Palatine and the Aventine Hills were constructed as part of Rome, though the Aventine Hill of Remus's choosing was always the grittier section of the two.

Afterward, Romulus set busily about setting up not only a grand city, but an ordered structure of government, and named the city after himself. The newly burgeoning city attracted lots of adventurous— and sometimes questionable—characters, mostly male. This led to an imbalance in the population, and the infamous raid of the Sabine women (see more on this in Chapter 13), which started Rome's first war, in which Romulus was ultimately victorious. Romulus went on to expand the territory of his city-state by amassing land, slaves, and peoples in many wars over many years. While many of his exploits were considered great, he was also sometimes reputed to be resented by the Senate that he had assembled as a form of government.

The death of Romulus is also disputed, as was his brother's death. Some accounts say that he simply disappeared, perhaps caught up in a great storm on one of his battle campaigns. Other accounts claim that witnesses saw him just suddenly ascend into heaven, presumably rewarded by the gods. Still, others contend that he was plotted against by the jealous Senate because he had taken too much power.

Whether Romulus and Remus were actual historical figures who became legendary over the passage of time, or whether they are entirely mythical, they are certainly still upheld as the founders of Rome. Some historians suggest that there might have been real people who inspired the larger myth, while others note that Aeneas himself wasn't even a figure of consideration until Emperor Augustus Caesar commissioned Virgil's epic many, many years past the foundation of Rome. Either way, the she-wolf remains a potent symbol of Rome, and the story of Romulus and Remus shows no signs of being discarded by the contemporary world.

CHAPTER 8: Epic Tales: The Aeneid

It would take far too long to tell the entirety of the ancient epic *The Aeneid*, but it is so essential to understanding the culture of ancient Rome, particularly the imperial phase, that it wouldn't do to leave it out. Essentially, this tale is as much—or more—of an origin story than the tale of Romulus and Remus. The epic is composed of twelve sections, and self-consciously mimics the great epics that came before it—*The Iliad* and *The Odyssey*, from the Greek tradition. It was commissioned by the first emperor of Rome, Augustus Caesar, in order to create a mythology that both glorified Rome and justified the Roman Empire itself.

Aeneas is a Trojan prince and a warrior-hero, albeit on the losing side, of the Trojan War. He escapes the city as it burns down, and sails the Mediterranean Sea in search of a new place to establish a homeland. The first half of the book concerns itself with the journey that Aeneas must take to find this home, while the latter half focuses on warfare and conquest. It paralleled many actual events in Roman history, such as the civil wars that erupted at the end of Rome's Republic before the establishment of the Roman Empire with Augustus Caesar. Caesar wanted a piece of public propaganda—and a great work of art—to justify the end of Republican rule, and glorify his imperial agenda and the Pax Romana (Roman Peace) that followed it.

The Aeneid begins, as epic convention requires, *en medias res*—in the middle of things. Aeneas and his men, after surviving the Trojan war, land on the shore of Carthage, a great Mediterranean city in the north of Africa. He is welcomed into the court of Queen Dido, and begins to tell his epic tale of battle, deception, and defeat. He relates his fear of the supposedly hollow horse that the Greeks bestow upon the city—the infamous Trojan horse. Aeneas was the only one to suspect trickery (heroes must be wise themselves); this episode is where we get the common platitude, "beware of Greeks bearing gifts," which colloquially implies that, if something looks too good to be true, it probably comes with strings attached.

In any event, the Trojan horse leads the Greeks directly into the city gates, and they are able to murder the king and burn the city. Aeneas and his men barely escape, and spend days sailing on the open Mediterranean sea, the point of the story being to highlight that Aeneas is a natural leader, and his men willingly follow him into danger—this would have direct parallels with how the Roman military would fight for their designated generals. Dido listens to Aeneas's story, rapt with attention, when she is struck by Cupid's arrow—Cupid happens to be Aeneas's half-brother. Their mother is Venus, of course. She immediately falls in love with Aeneas, who is, alas, a man on a mission, so he must leave her (more about Queen Dido in Chapter 13).

When he sets sail from Carthage, he goes to Cumae in southern Italy, where he seeks the priestess of Apollo, who guides Aeneas into the Underworld. This is a convention of epic poetry, the journey to the land of the dead, where the hero seeks answers to his destiny. He meets his deceased father, who predicts the greatness of Rome, and that its Golden Age will be commenced under the reign of a Caesar—an obvious reference to Augustus, who commissioned the work. This Caesar will be a direct descendant of King Ascanius, who was killed in the Trojan War, through the legendary Romulus, thus neatly weaving together two great foundational myths of Rome. This both serves to legitimize the new emperor's rule, and to retroactively predict the greatness of the Roman Empire: Of course, it is great, was great, and will be great, it was foretold.

Eventually, Aeneas and his men settle in the land of Latium, with the peaceful invitation of King Latinus, who has heard of Aeneas's great heroism and character. Aeneas intends to marry the king's daughter, thus cementing his inevitable succession to the throne. However, King Turnus of the neighboring peoples of Rutuli also seeks the daughter's hand, and when Aeneas is allowed to marry her, Turnus and his men take up arms against the fledgling kingdom.

Aeneas and his men are badly outnumbered, and he seeks help from other neighboring fiefdoms—that of the Tuscans and the Arcadians—for assistance. This series of events reveals how Aeneas is gifted at bringing disparate groups together; his bravery and heroism inspire others to unite behind him. Again, this would be a reminder to the Roman people that unity and military might are key to the successful founding and expansion of the empire.

Many bloody battles are fought and described in infinite detail. The epic ends—as certainly no one doubted it would—with the slaying of Turnus by Aeneas. Thus, the war is won; peace is established, and Rome can then begin its slow march to glory.

There are some central ironies to this epic story, still studied and talked about today. First, Virgil was unhappy with his work, and instructed his assistant to destroy it upon his death. Unfortunately, he died during the writing of a final revision, and Augustus was so pleased with it that it went out to the public as it was. Virgil, himself, was the greatest poet of the age, and his earlier works are still yet revered, as well (and they may, indeed, be better work—as art forms instead of propaganda).

What Augustus so adored about the work is that Aeneas was written as the ideal Roman hero—the ideal Augustan age man—both quick and decisive in action and steadfast in the preservation of a certain code of morality. Critics point out that the actual timeline is confounding, as about four centuries elapse between the Trojan War and the founding of

Rome. That is, Aeneas is not actually the great founder; instead, he is an idealized version of a man emerging from ignominious defeat to magnificent and legendary fame. As with the Greek epics that stand as models before it, *The Aeneid* celebrates the warrior spirit and the desire for a peaceful homeland. All great epic heroes seek two things: *Kleos* and *nostos*; to put it in the original Greek: Glory, and home.

CHAPTER 9: Epic Tales: The Metamorphoses

Next, we come to Ovid's magnificent set of tales, set from the time of the very creation of the world, to the death of Julius Caesar. It contains 15 books and more than 250 myths, many of which are well known, even if we aren't exactly sure of their origins. It was intended to be both a work of mythology and a book of history; it combines the two in a way that has become far less common in contemporary times. It is one of the most influential works in the history of Western literature, inspiring writers from Dante Alighieri to William Shakespeare and beyond. The *Metamorphoses* represents the triumph of a great poet following in the footsteps of the monumental Virgil and *The Aeneid*.

Ovid's work defies simple classification: It is an epic poem; it is a collection of fables, particularly of the animal variety; it is a mythological cornucopia of morality tales, emphasizing obedience to the gods. Of course, at its base, it is loosely held together by the action of metamorphosis—of the transformation of one thing into another. This weaves through the entire set of tales, from the very beginning creation story (that of chaos into the order of the universe) to the final tale of the death of Julius Caesar, which brought final order and peace after a civil war. This, too, serves to elevate Augustus Caesar who brought the Golden Age of peace to Rome—though he also brought imperial control and absolute power.

There are also many metamorphoses from humans into animals (the tale of Arachne and her weaving, for example: See Chapter 6 for more) and animals into humans. Most of these tales involve either obedience or disobedience toward the gods, resulting in reward or punishment.

The *Metamorphoses* also concerns itself with love, both erotic and platonic, which some scholars suggest is more prominently unifying than the title theme itself. Some of these myths were already familiar—such as the seduction of Io and her transformation into a cow—while others were fairly new, and Ovid gave his own particular poetic viewpoint to those stories. As with many works of Roman mythology, the *Metamorphoses* was profoundly influenced by the Greek tradition.

Among the many, many mythological stories recounted in Ovid's work, some of the more memorable are the tales of Daedalus and Icarus, Orpheus and Eurydice, and the Pygmalion. I choose these tales because they are the source material for numerous re-telling and re-workings throughout the history of Western literature and culture.

Daedalus was a skillful inventor and craftsman, who was commissioned to build the great Labyrinth for King Minos of Crete; this Labyrinth was intended to be a prison for the monstrous Minotaur of half-man, half-bull origins. When Daedalus had completed the

Labyrinth, Minos had him imprisoned in a tower—
with the reasoning that, if Daedalus told his secrets or
sold his abilities to other kings, then Minos would be
vulnerable. Since the king controlled all routes of
escape by land or by sea, Daedalus set about crafting a
pair of wings for himself and his son, Icarus, so they
might escape Crete. He warned his son not to fly too
high or too low: Too high, and the sun would melt
the wax that held the feathers together; too low and
the sea splash would soak the feathers, making them
too heavy to fly.

Icarus, in his giddiness at flying and his confidence in
his father's work, eventually began to soar higher and
higher, wherein the heat from the sun melted the wax,
as his father had warned. Icarus plunged to his death
in the sea. The moral of the story has often been
recounted as that of hubris: Icarus was so prideful in
the winged invention that he flew too close to the sun
and got burned. However, it might be that the
originally intended moral was that one must be

cautious of one's own inventions—the hubris was actually Daedalus', in that he did not take into account the dangers and consequences of his own brilliance. In the end, Daedalus bitterly mourned the loss of his son.

The tale of Orpheus and Eurydice is a different kind of tragic love story. As the son of Apollo, Orpheus was granted the gift of musical talent with the lyre (since Apollo was the god of music, this is no surprise). He plays so beautifully that he enchants the most beautiful young woman in the land, Eurydice. They marry, but it is prophesied that their happiness will be short-lived. Indeed, one day, Eurydice is out in the fields dancing with the nymphs, and is bitten by a venomous snake; she dies instantly and is whisked away to the underworld.

Orpheus, mourning his lover, decides to try to visit her in the underworld, braving the treacherous journey. But he plays his flute so beautifully that he gets by the three-headed dog guard, Cerberus, and even Hades, the god of the underworld, is enchanted and grants him a pass. He will be allowed to take Eurydice back to the world of the living—under one condition: Orpheus cannot look back until she is safely in the light. He cannot hear her footsteps behind him—she is still a shade of the underworld—and loses faith in the end. He looks back, only to see her vanish back into Hades' realm. The moral of this tale seems to be to obey the gods, to trust in them, or else suffer the consequences.

The myth of Pygmalion is rather short and sweet. Pygmalion was a gifted sculptor who carved the statue of a woman so beautiful that he fell in love with it. He made offerings to the goddess of love, and wished for a girl that was the living likeness of the statue he had made. When he returns to the statue and kisses her ivory lips, they begin to feel warm, and he realizes that his wish has been granted. In this tale, the simple moral is to make offerings to the gods, and in your piousness, your wishes will be granted.

Ovid's intention was to celebrate the variety and beauty of the Greco-Roman mythological tradition—and, of course, to cement his fame. He was already a renowned poet prior to his magnum opus; however, the success of *The Aeneid* was certainly something Ovid wanted to reproduce, in his own way. Unfortunately, Ovid ran afoul of Emperor Augustus, who wanted a return to traditional Roman morals, which he believed would strengthen an empire that had previously descended into chaos. Ovid pointed out that the emperor himself had committed many adulteries, as had his daughter Julia; basically, Augustus was enforcing this morality—with a penalty of death—upon the masses, but not upon the wealthy and powerful. So, Ovid was sent into exile until his death. Fortunately, his great work and the many mythologies within it survive with us today.

CHAPTER 10: The Senate: Rome as Democracy

From its mythological inception, Rome evolved from a set of tribal-style kingdoms into a Republic, following the Greek model. Strictly speaking, the Roman Senate is certainly not a mythological entity, but its origins and significance are so legendary that it behooves us to know something about it in order to understand the Roman culture of the time. In addition, we should not mistake the Roman Senate for Western-style democracy of the contemporary era; it was a body of privileged men who had some influence on how the politics of the day were carried out. This was still a revolutionary idea—that no single ruler or ruling family should hold absolute power. It is more revolutionary, still, when you remember that this proto-democracy flourished in an age of bloodthirsty conquests and within a city of slaves.

Rome was many things, but "simple" is not one of them.

The Roman Senate was not a body of elected members; rather, it was an advisory group of well-regarded (at least in most cases) men, appointed by counsels and magistrates. While there is some evidence to suggest that not all members were of the wealthy, ruling classes, it is certainly clear that this was most often the case. Legendary tradition says that Romulus himself created the first 100-member senate just after the founding of Rome. By the time of Julius Caesar, the ranks had grown to around 500.

Senators basically served for life, unless censured for some criminal or indecent doings; this did, in fact, happen with more frequency than one might suspect. It is equally true that many powerful senators, such as Julius Caesar, gave out appointments to those who favored him; in fact, it seems the Senate swelled to nearly 900 members at this time. When Augustus Caesar won the civil war that followed the exploits and death of Julius, he reigned in both the Senate's numbers and the Senate's powers.

Essentially, the main function of the Senate was to advise the various magistrates—and, later, the emperors, to increasingly futile effect—and to issue decrees and resolutions. Those decrees then became law if approved by the magistrates. Remarkably, even under the emperors, the Senate had the power to issue emergency decrees as deemed necessary to serve the stability of the state.

What is even more remarkable is that the Roman Senate represented an unparalleled moment in Western history, at the least, wherein a group of men decided to argue, debate, and ultimately compromise in order to do what was best, not for themselves personally, but for the larger commonwealth of the state. This is not to suggest that senators weren't corrupt, or didn't serve their own interests when they were in power, but it is to point out that, overall, the purpose and function of the Senate was to unify and keep safe an entire population working together, to create something magnificent. This was not how tribal groups worked; this was not how later medieval kingdoms would work. It was unprecedented cooperation among men to recognize the power of pleasing, rather than dominating, the lesser populations—again, to a degree.

The Senate even publically published a record of their proceedings—until Augustus put a stop to it. It seems that, in the heyday of the Roman Republic, the public itself had the right to know what its government was doing. The Senate was responsible for deciding on matters of public policy, such as the establishment of marriage laws and the implementation of financial institutions. It also debated areas of foreign policy and the creation of new provinces and borders. The rules of the Senate were complex and difficult, having been passed down from the earliest days of the republic, to the latter days of the empire. Still, the rule of law in the Republic of Rome was understandably unique in the ancient world. If you contrast that to the pharaoh-gods of ancient Egypt—with whom Rome had many dealings, both necessary and tragic—Rome was an enlightened democratic state.

In short, the Roman Senate was one of the longest continuously-operating institutions in the history of the Western world. While diminished under the imperial rule initiated by Augustus in 27 BCE, the Senate remained throughout the years of the empire. Ironically but shrewdly, Augustus recognized that maintaining the Senate kept up appearances that the Roman state was still a marginally-democratic one. He also quite rightly acknowledged that the Roman Senators were a powerful, and as such, dangerous, group of people, and his own power was at least partially contingent upon them. It can clearly be seen that the Greco-Roman influence on America itself is significant, from the design of the Capitol building in Washington, DC, to the body of elected members

that we turn to for legislation and the upholding of
the rule of law.

CHAPTER 11: The Emperors: Rome as Empire

The Roman Empire deserves its own thoroughly researched book—indeed, there are many—and encompasses many different periods and iterations. For the purposes of our overview of ancient Rome within this text, the focus will be on the beginnings of the Roman empire and into its expansion and height of power. Again, strictly speaking, the Roman Empire is a historical fact, not a mythological story, but it would be remiss not to discuss the empire—so important is it to understand the culture of Rome and the stories it produced.

The empire began in 27 BCE, when Augustus Caesar declared himself emperor after the death of Julius Caesar and the subsequent civil war that followed. Even prior to the transgressions and death of Julius, the Roman Republic had been steadily unraveling, for about a hundred years. There was economic stagnation and internal military disputes, as well as slave revolts from some provinces outside the main city-state. Perhaps the two biggest factors were the decisions made by Tiberius Gracchus, a young tribune (one of the ruling magistrates), to implement policy without the consent of the Roman Senate. In effect, Gracchus became the first "strongman" of the Roman Republic, and his decisions and autocratic style led to political dissension, as well as economic problems. The second was that of the dissatisfaction of the military: So many soldiers had served for so long in foreign conflicts that, when they came home, they found their land and farms taken by others. Basically, the army was at the point of revolt because their service to the empire did not count for much by the time they returned home. This internal crisis intensified for many years.

Julius Caesar, born of a very influential family, was able to capitalize on the sense of disenfranchisement in the military, and amassed several regimens of soldiers loyal to him. He was opposed by another influential soldier, Pompey Magnus, who also had troops loyal to him. Ostensibly, these were two generals in the army, and tribunes to Rome; in reality, both were vying for absolute power. Julius Caesar proved to be the better warrior—or at least had better luck—for he defeated Pompey, and, subsequently, declared himself dictator of the broken republic. As we know, he was murdered on the steps of the Roman Senate, leading to the civil war, and the success of his nephew Augustus Caesar, who declared himself emperor and embarked on a successful 40-year-long rule.

Under Augustus, the structure of the empire was laid out, as were its basic rules and regulations. For one, he nationalized the army so that it was loyal only to the Roman state, not to individual generals like Julius Caesar and Pompey Magnus. He also controlled the provinces and appointed the governors who oversaw them. The Roman Senate remained, but with much-diminished powers. Nevertheless, history still names Augustus's reign as a Golden Age in Roman history, and as he said himself, "I found Rome a city of clay and left it a city of marble." Indeed, part of his success was to increase prosperity and bring peace after more than a hundred years of uncertainty.

By 117 CE, about one hundred years after the death of Augustus, the Roman Empire reached its height as the most extensive political and cultural institution in all of the Western world. The "Five Good Emperors", as they are known, led Rome to expand its territories, increase its wealth, and establish order and stability throughout its realm. By 180 CE, at the end of the last of the Five Good Emperors, Rome began to see dissent and fractures in the empire: Constant wars with the "barbarian" tribes wearied and weakened the army; subsequent emperors became more corrupt and greedier; the influence of the Roman Senate waned further.

One hundred years after that, the empire still survived, but had grown so vast—a victim of its own ambition—that it was split into two: The Western Empire centered in Rome, and the Eastern Empire centered in modern day Turkey. This split eventually gave us the Roman Empire and the Byzantine Empire, which was ruled by Constantine some one hundred years after the split. His role is significant in that he converted to Christianity, and the two halves of the empire went their separate ways, politically and culturally. In addition, incursions by foreign forces into a weakening Rome eventually spelled doom— nearly five hundred years after its inception, the Roman Empire was no more.

Scholars debate the exact reason for the fall of the Roman Empire, but surely there are several competing factors: The split with the East, the rise of Christianity, the corruption of the rulers themselves, and the fading influence of the Roman pantheon of gods and goddesses. Certainly, the military, in the end, was spread too thinly to be able to defend from the invading Germanic tribes. The end of the ancient Roman Empire was official in 476 CE. The name lived on in the East for a time, but with little resemblance to what we talk about through this text: The pagan mythologies and traditions of the Roman religion were thoroughly and absolutely replaced by Christianity; the Byzantine Empire would survive until the fall of Constantinople in 1453; the Holy Roman Empire would be resurrected during the medieval period as a symbolic gesture to the earlier period of Roman power: The Pope's seat in Rome was served by associating itself with the legacy of one of the mightiest empires in history.

The legacy of the ancient Roman Republic and Empire is hard to overstate. Their advancements in technology, from indoor plumbing to paved roads and a sophisticated postal system, to their achievements in the arts—from visual art to architecture to literature, the Romans were unparalleled. But perhaps their most impressive legacy—one that allowed them to be great—was their ability to absorb and borrow from other cultures, to adapt to different influences, and to maintain a sense of what it meant to be Roman within a polyglot society. The Romans were, truly, the first "global" society, even if that term is limited to the Western world.

PART III: Monsters and Heroes

There cannot be great tales if there are no great foes or great heroes: This is the very stuff that myths are made of. All myths are stories of who we'd like to be and what we'd like to have—a form of wish fulfillment. They explain the world around us and the characters that populate that world. Heroes and monsters are beacons of light and darkness, of triumph and defeat, of right-thinking and wrong-doing. We gain insight into the culture that generates these various figures, learning their values, fears and hopes.

While monsters may function in mythology to provide obstacles to heroes, it is almost always the case that the monsters also work, symbolically speaking, to hold a mirror to ourselves: What we fear and what we despise usually arises from the lesser demons of our very own natures—that is, the monsters created in mythology represent our worst fears, our secret desires, and/or our least redeeming qualities. In ancient mythology, the monster typically represents the "Other": She, he or it is a manifestation of the direct opposite of what the teller of the tale values and holds dear. Because Greco-Roman culture did not have a vision of the end of the world, as did the Egyptians and the Norse, their myths do not have one primal enemy or one primal battle; the outlook on life was one of maintaining stability and order in the home and throughout the empire. In addition, monsters can be misread—or, certainly, re-interpreted—through time: The Minotaur and Medusa can be seen as victims of circumstances beyond their control, for example. The emperor-god Augustus Caesar is both a hero and a monster, depending on the circumstances. Sympathy for monsters may be a contemporary phenomenon, but it makes us think more deeply about our own cultural biases.

Heroes follow a similar pathway in most mythologies: He or she must undertake a journey, often perilous; on that journey, the hero must cross from the ordinary world, where the rules are understood, into an extraordinary world—the underworld, a supernatural realm, or even a foreign land—where the hero must use his or her wits to thrive. The hero faces a series of trials, sometimes with a band of allies, and must conquer his or her greatest challenge—the final test. If the hero overcomes it, then he or she will be granted some form of reward: Wealth and property; reputation and fame; security and companionship. Heroes represent the values that the society who tells his or her saga wants us to uphold—whether it be bravery in battle, or faithfulness in the face of temptation, or loyalty to those he or she loves. A hero is an ultimate representation of what society wants from its best members, and the values of a particular moment in time are often quite clearly revealed by what kind of hero that time creates.

Monsters and heroes speak to our personal psyches; we love to root for the good guy and take guilty pleasure in the defeat of the bad guy. This is one of the deepest pleasures of mythology—dreaming of being the great hero who is cheered on throughout history.

CHAPTER 12: Human-Animal Hybrids: Fiends and Friends

Human-animal hybrids exist throughout mythical and legendary tales throughout history. The ancient Romans had no monopoly on it: Think of our present fascination with werewolves and vampires— shapeshifters that are mainstays in popular culture. The mythological monsters that the Romans battled or befriended were, like much else in Roman mythology, derived from Greek sources. From the Minotaur to Medusa, these hybrid creatures were first described by the Greeks, and embellished upon by the later Romans.

Why the fascination with human-animal hybrids? Psychologically speaking, it is fairly clear that these part-human, part-animal creatures represent our dual nature: On the one hand, we are all rational, thinking humans; on the other hand, we often nurture (and usually suppress) a wilder, more animalistic side. This wild side can be both fearsome and freeing. It can justify a desire to harm others with no purpose, or it can allow us to dance in the moonlight and enjoy certain uncivilized delights. Animals are more closely aligned to nature, while humans are more closely aligned to culture. The portrayal of these hybrids vary, depending on how they are deployed in the particular mythical story they populate.

For one example, the legend of the Minotaur reverberates throughout Greco-Roman culture. The Minotaur is the half-man, half-bull offspring of a bestial affair, and, as such, is a monstrous abomination—a representation of uncivilized desire. King Minos of Crete was attempting to cement his somewhat tenuous hold on power—his brothers also laid claim to the throne—and boasted that he could appeal to the gods and they would grant him whatever he wanted, thus proving that he was divinely-ordered to rule. He prayed fervently to

Poseidon/Neptune, the god of the sea, to produce the most magnificent bull ever seen, and Minos would promise to sacrifice it.

When the bull actually appeared, however, it was truly magnificent, and Minos wished to keep it for his own. So, he substituted another bull in sacrifice, thus angering the gods. There was a love spell placed on Pasiphae, Minos's wife, driving her to lust unnaturally after the bull Minos refused to sacrifice. In the Greek version of the story, it is Poseidon who casts this spell in order to assert his supremacy. In the Roman version of the story, however, it is Venus, goddess of love, who so diabolically enchants Pasiphae, claiming that the woman had not shown proper piety to Venus. This highlights the cultural difference: The Roman emphasis on fidelity in marriage and propriety in women surely influenced the slight change in the story.

In both stories, Pasiphae is able to consummate her unnatural desire for the bull and eventually gives birth to the Minotaur. Minos is horrified by the evidence of his wife's monstrous affair, but does not, in fact, punish Pasiphae—perhaps realizing his own role in this betrayal. He hides the Minotaur away in the labyrinth and feeds it sacrificial subjects from the rival kingdom of Athens. The hero Theseus volunteers to serve as a tribute, and, so it was ordained, he was able to slaughter the hideous beast. Clearly, the myth serves several functions: First, it emphasizes obedience to the gods (Minos's error); second, it highlights the taboo against unnatural desire (Pasiphae's error); third, it provides a template for the creation of a new hero, Theseus. All heroes must prove themselves with great deeds, and the Minotaur was the occasion for Theseus to shine.

Another monster common to Greco-Roman mythology is the Medusa and her Gorgon sisters. There are several strands of the myth surrounding Medusa, with her famous hair of snakes and stare that could turn men to stone. Many stories simply describe her and her two sisters as fierce Gorgons with the ability to kill men. One version of the story suggests that Medusa was once a beautiful maiden who was raped by Neptune in the temple of Minerva. She punished Medusa (one wonders why) by turning her into a beast with snakes for hair and a serpent's tongue. Of the three sisters in the later telling, it was said that only Medusa was mortal. This provided, as the Minotaur did for Theseus, the stage for the creation of another hero, Perseus, who, by using cleverness and strength—and, lest we not forget, help from the gods—ultimately kills her. He uses his shield as a mirror to see where Medusa is, instead of looking directly at her, and is able to cut off her head. This story is played out over and over in literary history, visual art, and popular culture.

There are friendly creatures in the world of human-animal hybrids, as well. The god Bacchus is often surrounded by satyrs—half-goats and half-men—who represent the spirit of drunken freedom that is seen at the Bacchanalia. There are centaurs—half-horses and half-men—who are most often represented as civilized creatures with great wisdom that only bode ill if they become too drunk or too angry. These kinds of hybrids symbolize the cautionary tale that civilized humans can become less than such if they let their animal instincts take over, perhaps. Satyrs are friendly until their drunken desires cause them to assault maidens; Centaurs are friendly until their anger leads to confrontation. Note that the animals associated with fairly friendly hybrids are goats and horses, which provide much use to humans, while the bull and snake hybrids are frightening and powerful.

CHAPTER 13: Female Figures, Tragic Temptresses

The role of women in the ancient Roman world is complicated, as is much else in that complex civilization. Throughout history, women have been symbolic of society's best hopes and worst fears; they are often temptations to be avoided, vessels to be plundered, or monstrous manifestations of emotional excess. They can also be revered as wives and mothers, as virgins and upholders of the moral fabric of society. Roman culture designated the family as the center of society, so, in that sense, women were respected. Certainly, goddesses were worshipped for their feminine qualities. But they were also constant sources of fear and uncertainty. The representation of women in the mythology and legendary tales of ancient Rome varies widely.

Even in the foundational myth of Rome, there is a central female figure who invites both judgment and sympathy: Dido, Queen of Carthage. She was a legendary figure in her own right, a queen in her native land of Phoenicia until she was forced to flee. A loyal band of followers came with her and helped her found the great city of Carthage, in what is modern-day Libya. Her image was printed on the very coins Carthage used to trade; she inspired a great many followers, and Carthage became a city to be reckoned with in the ancient world. She is, indeed, a worthy foil for the hero Aeneas when he happens upon her shores.

However, when we see her finally in the epic story of Aeneas, Dido becomes a much different sort of woman. In *the Aeneid*, she has refused many suitors who come before Aeneas, but she is taken with his brave tales, and was struck by Cupid's arrow at the behest of Venus. She, therefore, falls deeply in love with Aeneas, and the two consummate their love in a cave at the shoreline. It is not to be, however, because Jupiter sends Mercury to remind Aeneas of his destiny: He must leave Carthage and sail to Italy to found what will become the greatest empire in the world.

As he tries to leave, he can hear Dido's mournful crying—indeed, her unhinged shrieking—for him to stay with her. He sails away anyway, and Dido leaps upon a funeral pyre, committing suicide in her grief.

Dido has come to symbolize much: First, she is the strong and capable leader of a great civilization, who is brought low by love. Second, she is the overly emotional—the word "hysterical," fraught with implication, comes to mind—and tragic female at the center of a male-dominated tale. Third, she is a nifty plot device in which Virgil, the author of *The Aeneid* can explain away the terrible Punic Wars between Carthage and Rome: Before Dido commits suicide, she pronounces a curse that there be an only war between the two peoples of Carthage and Rome. In this way, the poet tells his audience—the Roman people—that the brutal wars that were fought were pre-ordained, inevitable, and unavoidable—therefore, they were justified.

Another story of women faced with injustice at the hands of Roman men is the story of the Sabine women. Alternately called the *"Rape of the Sabine Women"* or the *"Kidnapping of the Sabine Women"*, it tells the story of the early days of Rome, when Romulus was still king. Because Romulus's followers were overwhelmingly male, there were no women with whom to start families and begin to populate Rome. Thus, they attempted to negotiate with the nearby Sabine tribe, to no avail. The Sabines rightly feared that the Romans would establish a rival society, a stronger kingdom, and then they would be extinguished. The Roman men were having none of this, so they planned a festival to which they invited many neighboring tribes—the Sabines included. Plotting a kidnapping, they waited until all the parties

112

were gathered, and, ignorant of the plot, enjoying themselves; Romulus gives a sign, and the men grab up the women and fight off the men. Romulus implores the women to accept their fate.

Some accounts suggest that the women themselves intervene in order to save the men of Sabine. Naturally, this account suggests that the women of Sabine take the blame for the attack, and thus must sacrifice themselves to the Romans to save their men and sons back home. Other accounts suggest that the Romans promised them more liberties and more prosperity, and thus they were seduced. It is almost certain that the earlier, more brutal recounting of the tale—abduction and rape—was whitewashed for the sake of later audiences, showing the Romans to be enlightened peoples, in comparison to their neighbors.

For the most part, women were certainly considered intellectual and emotional inferiors to men within ancient Roman culture. Their lives were dominated by men, from their fathers to their husbands to their brothers and their sons: All had rights before a woman in the family unit. Women were also held to higher moral standards than men—except in the upper classes—and could be punished for events that they could not control (such as rape). Women were objects of negotiation, functioning as symbolic unions between powerful families. Still, there were women who operated outside these boundaries of what was acceptable in polite Roman society. In any culture that keeps women fettered, there are scores of women who insist on defying the rules. Rome was rife with prostitutes who, if lucky, could make a better living than most poor women in the city. There are also stories of female gladiators—though the historical evidence is mixed—who fought in the arenas as a kind of novelty act. Whatever the case, the powerful Roman goddesses surely provide some evidence that Roman women, while perhaps constricted by law and custom, were surely not obsequious victims. The stories that survive are the only items we have by which to judge culture. And if these two stories above are any indication, women of the ancient world could be powerful—but, alas, they only had men to tell their tales.

CHAPTER 14: The Twelve Tasks of Hercules

Hercules is, undoubtedly, a hero for the ages: He was celebrated throughout the Pan-Hellenic world, and has been the inspiration for countless interpretations within popular culture, from the 90s television show, *Hercules: The Legendary Journeys*, to the Disney cartoon version, to a spate of recent films wherein Hercules is portrayed as the quintessential action hero (by Dwayne "The Rock" Johnson, among others). Hercules embodied virtually every heroic trait valued by Greco-Roman society. In fact, he is so larger than life—his exploits, his journeys, his multiple miraculous triumphs—that he was most likely a character who was the sum of multiple minor characters throughout the centuries. Lucky Hercules got to boast the name that pertains to them all.

Hercules, as with most other major characters in the Roman canon, was inspired or borrowed from the Greeks, where his legend got its start under the moniker "Heracles". His father was the king of the gods, Jupiter (or Zeus, in the Greek tradition), and his mother was a mortal. Thus, Hercules was a demi-god, and his origins explain his superhuman strength and abilities. Because Jupiter's wife was a jealous woman (though this is truer in the Greek tradition than the Roman), she made Hercules' life difficult from the beginning, sending snakes to kill him as an infant—not realizing that even the baby Hercules had the strength to strangle them. Nevertheless, for the most part, Hercules enjoyed the favors of the gods, and he was a particular acolyte of Minerva (Athena in Greek myths).

Hercules enjoyed an idyllic childhood, and was taught by some of the best teachers, so that Hercules was not only preternaturally strong, but also very clever and wise. Hercules eventually married and had five healthy children, which might have been the end of his story, had Juno (or Hera, in the Greek) not interfered. She was still angry at her husband's betrayal, and Hercules' happiness she could not abide. So, she drove him insane, and under her deranged influence, Hercules murdered his wife and all of his children. Desperate with remorse and wanting to atone for his sins, Hercules sought the advice of Apollo, who counseled him to be of service to his cousin, Eurystheus, the king of several mighty kingdoms. This advice was a mixed blessing at best: Juno/Hera once again interfered and convinced the king to set Hercules up with a variety of tasks that were almost certainly guaranteed to see him fail. However, Hercules' strength and intelligence would see him through. Thus, the infamous Twelve Labors of Hercules was born, initiating some of the most fanciful and adventure-filled mythical stories in the Greco-Roman canon.

His first task was to kill the Nemean lion, a creature whose hide was impervious to weapons; the lion was terrorizing the peoples of the region. The lion was no match for the strength of Hercules, and he was quickly dispatched by strangling. Forever after, Hercules wore his pelt for protection—and, of course, to display his heroism.

The second task was to slay the Hydra of Lerna, a monstrous amalgam of ferocious creatures with the head of a lion, and a body consisting of many snakes: Each time an opponent would cut off one snake's head, two would grow in its place. The Hydra was threatening the hometown of Hercules, and with a little help from his nephew, the Hydra was conquered: After each head was cut off, the stump was burned, preventing others from growing back. Hercules made sure to dip his arrows in the venomous blood of the Hydra. And a trend emerges: Each Herculean task makes Hercules stronger.

The third task was not to kill, but to capture the elusive hind sacred to Diana the Huntress: Hercules was to present it to the king unharmed. The hind was swift and capable, and as the myth has it, it took more than a year for Hercules to chase it down. Again, with each task, the myth and endurance of Hercules grew stronger.

The fourth task was to capture the boar of Erymanthian—a similar tale to the one above—emphasizing endurance. This task was marred by Hercules' inadvertent slaughter of the great centaur, Chiron: After Hercules defeated the boar, he dined with the Centaurs and asked for some wine. Thereupon, an enchanted cask was opened, and the intoxicating vapors captivated the wilder Centaurs, who were gathered around. Thus, a drunken brawl ensued, in which Hercules accidentally shot Chiron with one of his poisoned arrows. The moral behind this myth seems to be that the loss of control of one's humanity can lead to dire consequences.

The fifth task was to clean the Augean stables—perhaps the dirtiest job in the history of jobs. The herds of Helios were so vast that the cattle produced so much dung in a day that it couldn't possibly be cleared. Hercules—using his brains instead of his brawn on this task—dug tunnels around the stables, wherein he placed the waste and diverted them into the nearby rivers.

The sixth task ordered Hercules to kill the man-eating Stymphalian birds. Minerva (Athena) assisted Hercules by giving him noisy clappers with which to attract and distract the birds, thereby giving him the ability to shoot them down, one by one, with his arrows. The gods showed favor to this strong and witty man.

The seventh task is more complicated in terms of its mythological origins: Hercules was to kill the Cretan bull. As we already know, the Minotaur of Crete was kept in a Labyrinth by King Minos (see Chapter 12) and eventually killed by the hero Theseus. So, this attribution of Hercules suggests that the bull is either a different creature or that Hercules does not actually kill it but transports it to the Kingdom of Mycenae.

The eighth task was to capture the flesh-eating horses of Diomedes and give them to the king. The accounts vary, though some have Hercules feeding their master, Diomedes, to them in order to placate them into being led away to his cousin-king. This is potentially the inspiration for the ghoulish, yet helpful, thestrals in the Harry Potter series.

The ninth task was to steal the girdle of Hippolyta, the queen of the Amazons, the mythical race of female warriors that figure in certain ancient stories—and fostered the contemporary superhero myth of Wonder Woman. The underlying story here is that the Amazons are committed virgins, a society of women bound only to war and honor, not to men. To secure her girdle, Hercules had to seduce her; this part of the myth mostly remains unspoken, but it surely speaks not only to Hercules' power in battle, but to his finesse with women—a kind of proto-James Bond figure.

The tenth task was to round up cattle on the island of Erythia. The herd was protected by three monsters: Geryones of the three bodies, Orthos of the dog's head and serpent's tail, and a son of Mars, the God of War. This trio was still no match for the strength of Hercules, and this particular task created the Pillars of Hercules, the promontories that rise out of the Straits of Gibraltar. Hercules' legend had grown so strong, it could explain geological phenomena.

The eleventh task was to secure the apples of the Hesperides. The tasks were growing more difficult and complicated, and this one proved one of the most challenging. Hercules had to use his wits to figure out how to get the apples: He freed the Titan Prometheus in exchange for information on how to find the apples. The Titan Atlas, brother of Prometheus, said that he would show Hercules the way; however, Atlas was busy holding up the weight of the world on his shoulders. If only Hercules were strong enough to take his place, Atlas would get the apples. Naturally, Hercules was, and when Atlas returned, but was reluctant to retake his place as bearer of the world, Hercules tricked him into resuming his task and returned with the apples.

The twelfth and most difficult task was to capture the ferocious three-headed dog guardian of Hades, Cerberus. This tale may be the most involved of the twelve tasks, but suffice it to say that Hercules encountered many fallen heroes along the way, and ended up winning the task not through brawn, but through brain confidence: He captured Cerberus with no weapons at all.

Hercules' reputation as the greatest hero of the Greco-Roman world was secured, and he was granted immortality upon his death. With his induction into the Roman pantheon, he became a particular favorite of the Roman elite. Mark Antony considered him his patron god, as did some of the emperors. It is no small feat for one heroic figure to inspire devotion and artistic creation for centuries.

CHAPTER 15: Augustus Caesar and the Golden Age

It may seem odd to include an actual historical figure in a book about mythology, but Augustus Caesar is one of the most mythologized historical figures of any age: He declared himself Emperor of Rome—an unprecedented act—and was proclaimed a god when he died. History has alternately seen him as a hero—the savior of a Rome torn by civil war and economic hardship—and a monster. He was, indeed, a very harsh ruler in many ways, and some of his acts in the gaining and maintaining of power could be quite brutal. The Pax Romana that he ushered in was undeniably a time of peace and prosperity, though it came at the cost of the Roman Republic and the rights of many of his own subjects.

Octavian, as he was known prior to his ascension to power, was the nephew of Julius Caesar. Julius eventually adopted him, as he had no legitimate living heirs, and Octavian's father had died when he was very young. Indeed, Octavian was smart to embrace the name—he took on the "Caesar" name even before he was adopted—knowing that he could capitalize on Julius's great favor among the military. Mark Antony accused Octavian of owing everything to his name, rather than to his own talent.

After the assassination of Julius, Octavian allied himself with the famed general, Mark Antony, and they formed the Second Triumvirate, acting as co-regents of Rome, along with Lepidus. (The First Triumvirate of Julius, Pompey Magnus, and Crassus had fallen apart when Julius killed Pompey and seized power for himself.) Their first order of business was to hunt down and slaughter all those who had opposed Julius Caesar or who had actively participated in his killing. At the Battle of Phillipi, two years after Julius's assassination, Brutus and Cassius—the two main opponents responsible for the act—

were defeated by the Second Triumvirate, and ended their own lives. This was thought of to be an honorable death in ancient Rome, rather than to be captured.

After that initial triumph, Octavian and Mark Antony's relationship began to unravel. Lepidus had already been forced out of the Triumvirate because of his boasting and greed. With Mark Antony, the unraveling would be more complicated and bloodier. Octavian had given Antony his sister in marriage, hoping to strengthen their alliance. However, Antony had already fallen under the spell of the infamous Cleopatra VII of Egypt—he had begun an affair with her even before his marriage to Octavia. Eventually, Antony sued for divorce from Octavian's sister, which effectively ended their alliance.

Their dissolution was even more complex than a familial insult, really, for the two men were diametrically opposed in temperament and values. Antony thought nothing of affairs with women, and he scoffed at Octavian for protesting. Indeed, Octavian had already known about the affair with Cleopatra before the marriage, so there is some room to understand Antony's reaction. Octavian, for his part, came to believe that Antony's behavior was beneath that of a Roman, and that he had been corrupted by the foreign ways of the east—of Egypt. This made Antony, in Octavian's eyes, a feminized figure, less than a man, and ultimately not a true Roman any longer.

The final straw came when Octavian obtained Antony's will. It left vast territories to his own sons, and for a tomb to be built for himself and Cleopatra. Worse still, it declared that Caesarion—Cleopatra's child with Julius Caesar—be a true heir to Julius, rather than Octavian. The Senate revoked Antony's command, and declared war on Cleopatra. The decisive battle at Actium, more than a decade after Julius Caesar was assassinated, put Octavian in power for good. Antony and Cleopatra were both dead (the tragic story being the source of many re-tellings, most famously, in Shakespeare's play of the same name), and his troops had defected back to Rome. Octavian had both Caesarion and Antony's oldest son murdered. There was to be no challenge to his power now.

Calling himself Augustus ("The Illustrious One"), he now had supreme power over all of the Roman Empire. However, he was very careful not to make the same mistakes that Julius had: He did not declare himself dictator or emperor, but called himself "Princeps" (First Citizen), and kept the Senate intact for outward appearance. Indeed, he made a great show of pretending to resign his powers over to the Senate, having secured their loyalty; a cowed group after the chaos of civil war, they promptly granted him back his role as a leader. To the public, it appeared that the Republic was still functioning, though it soon became clear that the Republic remained so in name only.

Augustus assumed power in 27 BCE, and by 19 BCE, he was openly declared the supreme ruler. For all intents and purposes, Rome was now an empire ruled by an emperor. During his reign, Rome enjoyed unprecedented peace—which continued for many years after his death, in fact—and as a result of that peace, the economy began to flourish again. The arts also benefited, with many temples restored, new buildings constructed, and famous literary works commissioned (such as *The Aeneid*). Public works were also repaired or improved during that time; the public baths for which Rome is famous—indoor plumbing in the ancient world—were everywhere.

Augustus also changed laws regarding social norms, for good or for ill. Most notably, he passed many reforms regarding marriage, hoping to stabilize society from the ground up. He made adultery illegal— sometimes punishable by death—and providing financial incentives to families who had more than three children. There were also financial penalties for childless couples. The population of Rome would grow not by the influx of foreigners, but by the growth of true Roman citizens. In fact, these laws were inevitably harsher on women, and lessened the freedoms that women enjoyed under the republic. Augustus even had his own daughter and grand-daughter exiled because they had allegedly committed adultery. Remember, too, that women had no choice in who they married, so their well-being was not a matter of consequence for the men who decided these unions. Thus, adultery was common because marriages were political—not passionate—arrangements, for the most part.

Augustus died in 14 CE, and he was greatly mourned by his subjects, at least according to history. They did enjoy peace and prosperity under his rule, and their allegiance was certainly heartfelt for most. History has handed down two accounts of his last words: Officially, he said, "I found Rome a city of clay and left it a city of marble. "According to his adopted son, future Emperor Tiberius, he said, "Have I played the part well? Then applaud as I exit." Two very different versions fitting of a very complex man.

CHAPTER 16: Contemporary Characters: Roman Heroes of Pop Culture

Why are we still so fascinated with ancient Rome? The answer, of course, is manifold and obvious: Ancient Roman culture exerted undue influence on the Western world, in general, in our institutions, art and architecture, our literature, etc. In addition, besides the fantastic exploits of the military politics of the day, Rome boasted a massive archive of mythological stories and legendary heroes. Even the everyday culture of Rome has sparked fascination: The gladiator continues to be an omnipresent source for entertainment today; at least, now, he is not fed to the lions—just the critics. One could argue that the foundations for European and, by extension, American culture had its roots in the soil of Greco-Roman history (along with other influences such as

Christianity, of course). We are still entertained by these myths, by this history, because it feels both familiar and foreign at the same time.

There is also, lest we forget, a strong connection to the military aspect of this history. America has always been a country dedicated to, and somewhat defined by its military; the past two decades of conflict in foreign countries has only heightened our connection to the great generals and heroes of times past. Certainly, America has always loved a rough-and-tumble hero ready to prove himself in battle; the number of movies that glorify this is staggering. We also tend to love the underdog, which is why we get Roman themed films like *Spartacus*, wherein the slave-turned-gladiator engineers a revolt against the empire that wronged him. Or, *Gladiator*, with Russell Crowe as a simple soldier who was denied his chance to return home and forced to defend his life in the arena. These stories are appealing—if tragic, ultimately—because the ordinary person is thrust into the role of

135

an unlikely hero and showed bravery beyond what we can reasonably expect. We like to see ourselves in these roles; like to think that we would be able to perform such great acts if put to the test.

In addition, the images of ancient Rome are resplendent; the costumes fantastic: The Coliseum looming above the skyline, the chariots roaring through the arena, the regalia of military dress, the helmets, and swords, and shields, are all irresistible. HBO's series *Rome* makes excellent use of not only these traditional clichés, but also reveals the underbelly of Rome, showing what it was like to be a plebian—a common citizen—in the many neighborhoods of Rome. The series itself follows the exploits and death of Julius Caesar throughout the war between Octavian and Mark Antony. Egypt gets its fair share of screen time, too. Historically accurate, for the large part, and lavishly filmed, it is a wonderful visual representation of what ancient Rome might have been, though it is meant for mature audiences only.

The figure of Cleopatra, too, has become an easily-identifiable cultural icon. The image of Elizabeth Taylor in the 1963 movie of the same name is exotically gorgeous (though the movie itself gets very mixed reviews). Indeed, the story of Antony and Cleopatra has fascinated writers and entertainers for centuries, starting with Shakespeare. A quick internet search shows almost two dozen films that focus on Cleopatra, though none were made recently.

Indeed, there are dozens of films, hundreds of literary treatments, and innumerable representations in other media that bring us the images of an ancient Rome, whose power is still in full force.

CHAPTER 17: Other Enchanting Stories & Figures

As one can easily imagine, this set of stories has merely scratched the surface of what's available in the canon of Roman myth and legends. Remember that the Roman peoples eventually covered a vast area and encompassed many different cultures, so there are innumerable legends and tales about innumerable gods and heroes, goddesses and enchantresses, monsters and foes. Roman mythology also clearly reverberates even today, as we have seen throughout our times, influencing popular culture in many ways, large and small.

There are so many myths within the Greco-Roman canon that it would be difficult to recount them all in one place. Some other enchanting stories that one could further investigate include the following:

- *Jupiter and the Bee*: This parable tells of a bee who is irritated by humans stealing her honey, so she appeals to Jupiter for help. She asks him to grant her a stinger, so she may harm any who try to take her honey. Jupiter was displeased with this request, for he was fond of humankind—at least at the moment of this story—so he grants her request, but with a dire caveat: When she stings, she, herself, will die. Clearly, the author(s) of this myth was cautioning against the dangers of wishing harm on others while doing good for yourself.

- *The tragedy of Cassandra*: Cassandra was a beautiful young woman who had attracted the attention of the god, Apollo. She refused his advances until he promised to grant her the power of prophecy, so she agreed and was given this power. Then, she decided to refuse Apollo anyway, and he cursed her so that nobody would ever be able to understand her prophecies. It was she who prophesied that the Trojan War would end in disaster, but Aeneas and the others could not understand her warnings—thus the tragedy ensued.

- *Pluto and the River Styx*: the god of the underworld, Pluto had to guard his keep well. Cerberus, the three-headed dog, stood to watch at the gates, but there was also the treacherous River Styx that one had to cross, too. If one came in contact with the river, it was said that one's voice would be lost for nine years.

There were also many legendary figures in actual ancient Roman history, as we have seen throughout. The Caesars, Mark Antony, Cleopatra, and others loom larger than life. Some other figures of note include the following:

- Emperor Nero: Legend has it that this exceedingly terrible and greedy emperor played his fiddle while he passively watched more than half of Rome burn. His name has become shorthand for the dismissive way that the wealthy and powerful treat the masses.

- Commodus: Played by Joaquin Phoenix in the movie *Gladiator*, Commodus is another example of one of the bad Roman emperors. His father, Marcus Aurelius, was considered an excellent military tactician, and is remembered today for his stoic philosophy. His son, however, was a bit unhinged, pretending to be Hercules, and generally behaving the fool. He was eventually killed by members of his own inner circle.

- Emperor Trajan: The first emperor of non-Roman descent, Trajan was a Spaniard who had proven himself on the battlefield and became so Romanized that he eventually held the title of "emperor". Trajan's Column can still be seen in Rome, detailing the many victories that he had won throughout his years as a general. He was also a benevolent emperor, handing out food and funds to the poor.

- Gaius Marius: Considered to be the first great general of the Roman army, Marius was able to turn the military into one of the most effective fighting bodies in history. His emphasis on discipline and inclusion— allowing provincial men from outside Rome to serve—surely saved the republic from the earliest barbarian incursions.

- Marcus Cicero: A great senator and orator, for much of what we know about ancient Rome at the time of Julius Caesar. He was not only a statesman, but also a philosopher and master stylist. Indeed, his manner of writing was copied, up until the 19th century.

These are merely a few of the many dozens of other captivating stories, myths, and legendary figures that you can find from ancient Rome. It is truly a wondrous source of inspiration and fascination.

Conclusion

There is nothing quite like the power of myth to move us to think about other people and places. The legendary feats of heroes, the dastardly deeds of monsters and sometimes gods, and the sweeping scope of epic tales, all draw us into a different world. Myths serve a crucial purpose: They function to remind us of who we are, and how we should (and should *not*) behave. They also explain the world to peoples before the advent of science and technology, creating comfort in times of strife and scarcity.

Roman mythology is unique, in that the people who created these tales and the practitioners of the attending religious beliefs were also the peoples who became a part of one of the greatest—if not the greatest—empire in history, spreading its cultural influence throughout the world and throughout Western history. Thus, Roman mythology is bound by certain motifs—the significance of the soldier-state;

the inherent human quality in all beings, supernatural or not; the importance of territory and reputation— that appear throughout the canon. Ancient Roman mythology was not, unlike other older mythologies, significantly impacted by the later Christianization of their territory as the empire continued into Christendom; the older material was rediscovered during the Renaissance, and were left mostly intact, serving as a reminder for a different way of life. This serves to highlight the grandeur of Roman mythology and its truly epic scope—hence, its continuing widespread appeal.

Hopefully, as you reach the end of your journey here, you take up new roads to learn more about other traditions and tales mentioned throughout the ebook. A new telling of ancient Roman culture and mythology have captivated our current popular culture, so should the original tales likewise demand our fascination.

Connect with us on our Facebook page

www.facebook.com/bluesourceandfriends and stay tuned

to our latest book promotions and free giveaways.

Lightning Source UK Ltd.
Milton Keynes UK
UKHW010733011220
374435UK00002B/545